SEARCH AND RESCUE

JOSHUA SAGE

SEARCH AND RESCUE

WRITTEN BY
JOSHUA SAGE

COPYRIGHT (C) 2020

ISBN: 978-978-985-991-7

COMMUNE WRITERS INT'L

www.communewriters.com

+234 813 926 0389

Published by:

Printed in the Federal Republic of Nigeria

CONTENTS

DEDICATION

To Almighty God the Father, Christ the Son, and the Holy Spirit of God - all glory and honor.

To true believers in Christ everywhere across the globe - may the Lord strengthen and keep you!

To Christian Atheists, Nominal, and Cultural Christians around the world - we see and appreciate you, there is a reasonable validity in your anchoring to Christianity; I hope this book brings you closer to God and His transcendent truth.

To my family, especially my mother and my sister who graciously fed, encouraged, and critiqued me while I wrote - a gazillion thanks.

To all my friends and church families - a zillion thanks.

FOREWORD

The relationship between Christ and the church, and every Christian, is like that of the Husband and His bride; and as brides of Christ, our relationship with Him is null if we ignore, avoid or alienate His family (His followers, the church, fellow Christians, the needy and the helpless) His likes and dislikes, His hobbies and preferences.

Every relationship has its boundaries and allowances. Religion - as delineated in the New Covenant of the Bible - true before God provides the structure, sets the boundaries, and affords us allowances in our relationships with Christ.

INTRODUCTION

"Religion that God our Father accepts as pure and faultless is this: to look after orphans and widows in their distress and to keep oneself from being polluted by the world." (James 1:27)

Over the last few decades (or centuries), the concept of religion has received sharp criticism, tarnished imagery, and bad publicity - in many cases deservedly so! One only needs to read or listen to the likes of Christopher Hitchens and Richard Dawkins and their vicious pontifications on the numerous atrocities done in the name of religion.

Christians nowadays are pressured from within and without to "lose their religion", ranging from quiet internal pressures like Kirk Franklin's album Losing My Religion, the New Apostolic Reformation (NAR) movement, and the New Age Spirituality to the bombshell grenades of popular Church scandals and prevalent religion-related acts of terrorism perpetrated in several parts of the world today.

It is important, however, to note that these atrocities were committed in the name of and under the guise of religion, sometimes amounting to the abuse of said religion. Even if they were outworkings of religions as they sometimes are, the Encyclopedia of Wars estimates that less than 10% of all wars are due to religion. The rest are due to power, oil, land, capitalism, communism, nationalism, tribalism, among others…but we do not see any large-scale movements to lose any of these, except maybe communism.

What Christianity suffers from, in my opinion, is guilt by association and abuse. The late Ravi Zacharias loved to often say, "You cannot judge a worldview by its abuse." By abuse, Christianity is declared guilty when we look to issues like the catholic Church scandal, the gay reformation camps, and the infamous crusades - clear cases where there was an abuse of the Christian doctrine.

By association, Christianity is grouped with other religions and when the wrongs associated with religions are considered, it is convicted alongside the group. Ravi also loved to say, "one should not throw away the baby with the proverbial bathwater." I dare say, pick up the baby, throw away the dirty bathwater, cloth the baby, let the baby do great things, and when the baby inevitably gets dirty, return to the bath, wash, rinse, repeat.

Regarding Christianity as just another religion is like referring to a car as 'wheels' - a simple and sometimes misleading synecdoche. Religion, like wheels in a car, is a part of Christianity but not the whole of it. Christianity is a way of life consisting primarily of a relationship with Christ, the religion of Church, Charity, and Chastity.

Relationship with:

- Christ, the Father, and the Holy Spirit (John 14:23),

Religion of:

- Church - gathering with other believers (Hebrews 10:25),
- Charity - loving one another, loving others, and helping all who need it (John 13:35), and
- Chastity - keep oneself unspotted from the world. (James 1:27)

Many have also attempted to propose that Christianity is not a religion, due to the baggage that comes with the term. This is understandable, but not optimal. Religion is the universal descriptive term for any cultural system of morals, attitudes, views, and daily practices. It encompasses worldviews, sacred texts, sacred places, and organizations that connect people to the supernatural.

To say Christianity is not a religion may be an attempt to deny reality, it is more apt to say that Christianity is a religion like no other. William Shakespeare wrote, "that which we call a rose by any other name would smell as sweet." And I say to you, "that which we call Christianity by any other name would still be, and function as a religion."

The Christian religion differs significantly from other religions in that it does not initiate the connection to God, but is a result and means of maintaining an already established connection and relationship with God - like a pipe to water - shaping, guiding, propelling, propagating it out into the world from the Source. In Christianity, Only God can connect man to God and establish a relationship that leads believers to religion, but religion will not get believers to God. Christians do not have to lose their religion or detach it from their relationships with God, because relationship (Faith) without religion (Works) is dead!

Movements against religion are brilliant assaults in a bigger war against God; other than being spiritual, they are battles of rhetoric, ideas, words, and opinions in a war for supremacy. Christians should be on guard to resist the forces within and without. Using acronyms of seven popular intelligence agencies and three tactical movies as mnemonics, I hope we can continue to be prepared and equipped to withstand the adversarial and accusatory antics of the Enemy.

CHAPTER ONE
FBI (FAITH BASED IDEOLOGY)

The Christian worldview is primarily an FBI, a faith-based ideology. This implies that it is built on good confidence in contrast to Cartesian certainty, or absolute knowledge. Like the real FBI, the Christian FBI serves to inform, protect, and defend the Christian community.

Faith plays a very important role in the life of a Christian. Ephesians 6:16 says, "In all circumstances take up the shield of faith [part of the Armor of God], with which you can extinguish all the flaming arrows of the evil one."

- Faith is the believers' defense and protection (It is God, but one needs to have faith in Him to call on His protection).
- Faith is a part of believers' law enforcement because it is the faith in a supreme lawgiver that enables adherence to such law.
- Faith also provides leadership and scrutiny to other aspects of a Christians' life - the level of faith determines prayer life, meditation, evangelism, etc.
- Faith, like the FBI, is also that which initiates and facilitates a searchlight into the believers' religiosity and relationship with God.

"Now faith is the assurance of things hoped for, the conviction of things not seen." (Hebrews 11:1)

There is a popular and erroneous misconception that Faith is believing in something without evidence. The Hebrew and Greek words usually translated as faith in the Bible can mean faith, trust, belief, confidence, religion, devotion, and support. Most Christians will define faith today as trusting in something or someone that we have good reasons (evidence) to believe in.

People can sometimes get stuck on the phrase, 'conviction/evidence of things not seen'. This is usually not warranted as many of us have never seen the things we believe and have faith in, like love, gravity, the moon landing, micro-organisms, numbers, laws of logic, thoughts, the British civil war of the 1770s, and many others. We believe and have faith in these things because we have good reasons to do so, not because we have seen them with our own eyes.

Another common stumbling block is the concept of believing without seeing. In John 20:29, Jesus said to Thomas, "Have you believed because you have seen me? Blessed are those who have not seen and yet have believed." This is mere rhetoric as Thomas had enough evidence from friends and family, yet still did not believe - John 20:24-25, Thomas was not with them when Jesus appeared. So, the other disciples told him, "We have seen the Lord." But he said to them, "Unless I see... I will never believe." Not many persons require visual proof when they have the testimony of trusted family members and friends.

Last on this list of popular polemics – purported points - is the passage in 2 Corinthians 5:7 that says, "for we walk by faith, not by sight." Considering what has been laid down above, it is only fair to simply note that none of us have seen tomorrow, but because today happened, we save and sleep and prepare for something we have never seen.

Married couples copulate, and some even name their children before conception. To say that conception and childbirth are scientifically proven buttresses to the point being made; most parents did not watch a couple make love or watch cells fuse before they ventured to make their babies. They heard about it from others, in classes, scientific studies, and media illustrations. In other words, they learned about it from individuals who told them in different ways: they walked by faith, not by sight.

Deploying The FBI

- The Church as it is today is not perfect, it is not supposed to be. Instead, it is supposed to gravitate towards perfection, reaching it when Jesus comes. So when we have grievances within the body of Christ or we see something we feel should not be the case - we must remember to employ and deploy the FBI (Faith-Based Ideology), persevere like the Patriots quarterbacks, and be active parts of the change for good.

- When people - within or without - cite the failings of religion either as a whole or in particular to try and convince us to abandon the Christian religion, we should accept the criticisms and politely explain that we will work with the FBI. The Christian religion is different from other religions and has shown a history of cleaning itself up periodically, therefore we must be ready to be a catalyst for that clean-up if need be!

- When confronted with rhetoric and polemics like those discussed, we gracefully tell them that we have checked with the FBI, and neither faith nor the Christian religion is what they proclaim it to be. We as Christians have good reasons to believe, trust, and have faith in God. Find yours!

- Whenever we inevitably face personal struggles, sometimes these are allowed for us to grow (we tear muscles to make them stronger). Kindly stay in touch with the FBI. If God has brought us this far, he can carry us even further. Do not give up on God, He is with you in all situations and will help when you call Him. He is God, He is able.

CHAPTER TWO
NSA (NOT SAVED ALWAYS)

The NSA should rightfully be a part of every believer's life, home, and church. This stands for Not Saved Always because our salvation is very precious to us and not to be played with. We must engage in constant monitoring and processing of signals, information, and data to ensure the integrity of the salvation given to us by Grace. We do not earn our salvation, but we get to keep it or lose it.

While Churches, fellowships, and family units are enjoined to look out for one another, the believer is the one-person agency tasked with the integrity of their religion and the maintenance of their soul's salvation. Like the real NSA, the believer needs to watch out for both domestic and foreign counterintelligence, using the Holy Spirit to filter actionable intelligence by testing all spirits, messages, and doctrines.

In Christian history, several doctrines emerge over time - the good, the bad, and the ugly. Some of such doctrines often find their origins in people who extrapolate a few bible verses to support non-Christ-like beliefs or behaviors. The dangerous counterintelligence discussed in this book is the doctrine of 'Once Saved, Always Saved' (OSAS).

This doctrine of OSAS finds its main root in John 6:39, as Jesus said, "This is the will of the Father who sent Me, that of all He has given Me I should lose none but should raise them at the last day." and a floating root in Revelations 7:4, where John reports, "And I heard the number of the sealed, 144,000, sealed from every tribe of the sons of Israel". OSAS teaches that if Jesus will not lose anybody that God has given to Him and there are those 'sealed' of the tribes of Israel - once believers are saved, God gives them to Jesus and He will not lose any of them, after all, none can break the seal of a king in his kingdom. Ergo, once saved, always saved.

What this doctrine fails to take into consideration includes the following:

- The passage in John expresses the will of the father, not His order or commandment. Christians know that it is also the Father's will that all men be saved, but a sad reality that this will likely not be the case.

- Jesus, when reporting to God and praying for the disciples in John 17:9-12, He says, "...those (disciples) whom You gave me I have kept; and none of them is lost except the son of perdition, that the Scripture might be fulfilled." This means that sometimes after Jesus said the

Father's will was that He should not lose anyone He was given, He lost one of twelve.

- Paul, a contemporary of Christ, urges believers in Philippians 2:12 to, "...work out your own salvation with fear and trembling," if salvation is sealed, there would be no need to work out anything with anybody.

- The Raising up on the last day mentioned in John 6:39 could very well include the saved and the unsaved, to stand before God in judgement. This would imply that Jesus would not have lost anyone He was given, at least not until after the last day.

Deploying The NSA

- Watchful Vigilance - Being vigilant and watchful for false teachings and doctrines. Now that we are acquainted with NSA, we are obliged to monitor, gather, and process doctrines coming to nest in our area of purview. We should note the signals and red flags. Before taking any affirmative action, we must report to God in prayer and constantly check with our agency's operation manual, The Holy Bible (reliable translations).

- Domestic Danger - One may find groups or individual believers who become delinquent and almost lackadaisical in their walk with God, carrying the torch of the OSAS doctrine and propagating its smoke. We should activate the NSA (Not Saved Always) immediately and utilize the Informal Resolution System (IRS) by trying to approach them and reconciling the matter at the lowest level possible. If this does not work, we take the matter up the chain of command (elders, leaders, God - in no particular order - involving God in all steps).
- Hybrid Danger (Insider Threat) - Due to the imperfection of the Church today, conflicts will arise, and upholders of OSAS may advise the griever(s) or grieved party to simply leave the

congregation, and probably stop bothering about believers' assembly altogether since it does not affect their salvation according to OSAS (lie from hell). Once again, with love, patience, and understanding, we are to deploy the NSA by explaining the scriptural message and praying with them and for them relentlessly, so help us God.

- Foreign Danger - Unbelievers who are either informed or were believers of OSAS will sometimes confront believers with the problems of the OSAS doctrine, showing how it is inconsistent, does not make sense, and could be potentially dangerous to society. They may do this to ridicule a believer, to prevent a non-believer from believing, or to pluck a believer from the fold of Christ. In this case, we can show our NSA badge, using the scriptures to explain that Christianity does not teach "Once Saved Always Saved."

CHAPTER THREE

CIA (CONTINUOUS IMPROVEMENT AND ASSESSMENT)

Organized CIA, Continuous Improvement and Assessment is an invaluable asset to the body of Christ. The body of Christ - Church and believer alike - is tasked with gathering, processing, and analyzing mainstream and feedback information from around its immediate environment. The utility of continuous CIA cannot be overstated.

Contrary to widespread opinion, the Christian lifestyle is a very dynamic, very fluid, and anti-dogmatic way of life. As Christians we must always be checking and rechecking ourselves by gathering and analyzing intelligence from outside sources, updating as needed. Thankfully, we can always get feedback from the Church body, from the Word of God, and directly from the Holy Spirit.

This book provides a starting point for activating individual SACs - Self Assessment Centers - by entreating readers to an appetizer course of the rich abundance of CIA tools in the bible, readers should consult the scriptures for more examples:

- Therefore, if anyone is in Christ, he is a new creation; old things have passed away; behold, all things have become new. (2 Corinthians 5:17)
- Do not be conformed to this world, but continuously be transformed by the renewing of your minds so that you may be able to determine what God's will is—what is proper, pleasing, and perfect. (Romans 12:2)

- Study to show yourself approved unto God, a workman that needs not to be ashamed, rightly dividing the word of truth. (2 Timothy 2:15)

- All Scripture is given by inspiration of God and is profitable for doctrine, for reproof, for correction, for instruction in righteousness, that the man of God may be complete, thoroughly equipped for every good work. (2 Timothy 3:16-17)

- Be on your guard and stay awake. Your enemy, the devil, is like a roaring lion, sneaking around to find someone to attack. (1 Peter 5:8)

- Therefore, be on the alert, for you do not know which day your Lord is coming. (Matthew 24:42)

- See, I am doing a new thing! Now it springs up; do you not perceive it? I am making a way in the wilderness and streams in the wasteland. (Isaiah 43:19)

Deploying The CIA

- Civil - The CIA is civil(ian), we should always engage in civil continuous improvement and assessment. We should also use the CIA when being faced with the confrontation of dogmatic belief in any form or manner, to simply learn more about ourselves and God, and to grow our faith and better ourselves in Him.

CHAPTER FOUR

MI6 (MITIGATING I-6)

Christians should especially be on the lookout for the MI6, the Mitigating I- 6. This stands for six mitigating situations or circumstances that start with the letter I. These situations are Infiltration; Intermission; Interference; Interruption; Interpolation and Insubordination.

Watching out for the MI6 serves the purposes of counterterrorism, counter-proliferation, spiritual integrity, and the disruption of spiritual acts of terrorism in our Christian lives, homes, Churches, and communities. Knowledge of the MI6 helps mitigate situations that stand to derail everything a Christian stand for. These phenomena are also tools used by anti-God and anti-Christian elements, usually dressed up as something other than they are:

INFILTRATION - This is the act of entering or gaining access to an organization or place surreptitiously, especially to acquire secret information or cause damage. An ancient Yoruba adage says, "If the wall does not open its mouth, the lizard cannot get into the wall". While the Church must remain an open door for all and sundry, anything or anyone that seems too neutral, too good to be true, or probably not expedient should be subject to rigorous and appropriate verifications.

INTERMISSION - This is a pause or break in production or process. Christians should be on high alert whenever the Holy Spirit appears to often stop working among them; we serve a God who neither sleeps nor slumbers. This intermission in the Spirit moving can be a clear sign of becoming lukewarm or worse. This could also be the sign of a break in the chain of connection to the divine - Joshua and his people suffered from Achan's breakage from the covenant (Joshua 7:1). Christians should always examine their relationship with God.

INTERFERENCE - This is the act of preventing a process or activity from continuing or being carried out properly. In physics, interference is the combination of two or more electromagnetic waveforms to form a resultant wave in which the displacement is either reinforced or canceled (sounds ominous). Even when the Children of God are gathering in God's court in the book of Job, Satan was among them. Detractors and enemies of progress show up in Church gatherings, these have nowhere to go but they prevent others from getting anywhere. Better equipped to deal with this are people in Church leadership positions. There are also detractors outside of Church - human and non-human (games, entertainment, etc.), these prevent the Spirit of God and His will from continuing or executing properly in the life of believers. Any form of interference should be neutralized as quickly as possible. (1 Timothy 6:4-5)

INTERRUPTION - Interruption represents the stoppage or hindering of activity for a significant amount of time, a break in continuity - synonymous with discontinuity. The Church's purpose includes being a conduit for God's activities. After many intermissions, interferences, and possible large-scale infiltrations, the activity of the Spirit will most likely become interrupted, hindered, and discontinued. The bible explains that God's Hand is not short, but our actions and inactions determine His workings amongst us. (Isaiah 59:1-2)

INTERPOLATION - This is the act of inserting something of a different nature into something else, to alter or corrupt by inserting new or foreign matter. This is evident today with the enormous pressure on the Church to adopt certain practices and ideologies that are not based in the Bible. The Church must resist, if even with Its last breath (Glory awaits those who persist till the end). Earlier chapters briefly dealt with the dangers of false doctrines, which is a form interpolation, other forms of interpolation are:

- Introducing worldly antics into the Church.
- Incorporating ideas from other religions/philosophies into Christianity.
- Adding, removing, or twisting the word of God to suit selfish purposes.
- False prophecy, fortune telling, blasphemy against the Spirit, etc.

INSUBORDINATION - If one clause or phrase could sum up Christianity, it would be "obedience to YAHWEH". Insubordination is the defiance of authority; a refusal to obey orders or instructions. Proverbs 16:18 records, "Pride goes before destruction, and a haughty spirit before a fall." Sustained, insubordination will sever (not just prevent, stop or block) any relationship with God. God is patient and longsuffering; however, His hand of protection is repelled at every instance of insubordination. God may give such subordinates up to their desires, remove His hand of protection over them, replace them, and when their cup is full, release judgement upon them. (Hebrews 10: 26-31; Matthew 3:9)

Deploying the MI6

- Prevention is better than cure, now that we know these six I-words, we can stay informed, and keep updated, "...so that we would not be outwitted by Satan; for we are not ignorant of his designs." (2 Corinthians 2:11)

- Resist the devil and flee all appearances of evil - Circumstances where the ears of the people are being tickled and they do not want truth can bring believers to ruin and the church to desolation. Christians are to remove themselves from such gatherings and/or remove the dangerous elements. (James 4:7; 1 Thessalonians 5:22)

- The MI6 dominates in areas of covert operations. The six phenomena discussed can present in various deceptive forms, including but not limited to the following ways:
    - Infiltration is often dressed up as inclusiveness,
    - Intermission and interruption are renamed as 'spirit downtime',
    - Interference is cloaked as 'mysterious ways' or 'regular life stuff',
    - Interpolation is disguised as progressiveness and,
    - Insubordination is hailed as critical (non-normative) thinking. BEWARE!!!

CHAPTER FIVE

DEA (DON'T ENTERTAIN APOSTASY)

DEA, standing here for 'Do not Entertain Apostasy', is crucial for maintaining sobriety and coherence in Christian living. We have learned in previous chapters; how internal and external factors can easily lead to the falling out and backsliding of believers.

As Christians, we are implored to resist apostasy fiercely and firmly. It used to be the case that exile, excommunication, and death were penalties for peddling the drugs of false gods and practices in the old covenant. It may sound like overkill, but a community infested with drugs is a community with stunted growth, retardation, crime, and poverty; the same is true for a church infested with seeds, plants, fruits, or other elements of apostasy.

Apostasy here will be expanded to mean the abandonment of core Christian religious beliefs and the adoption of false practices. Apostasy, like illegal drugs, easily besets and can be dangerously addictive. The Church and believers are admonished to review, retire, and realign various positions and beliefs that may have been misguided as they grow in the knowledge of God. Some beliefs are primary edicts from the unchanging God that make up the core of the Christian faith - Jesus, when asked about divorce, referred back to the beginning and other of creation to emphasize God's original purpose for marriage! (Matthew 19:1-8); others are secondary positions - Jesus, at the well in Samaria, predicted and reviewed temple or mountain worship. (John 4:20-21) Our bodies have since then served as God's temple!

Apostasy comes in several forms, shapes, and sizes:

- One of the most dangerous ones are those leading away from the congregation of believers. The benefits of a Church home overwhelm, this is evidenced by the trials and failures of non-religious churches in several places. There is growth, encouragement, belonging, opportunity, family, support, safety, relationship, fellowship, and more in the Church community. Mankind is a social creature, never meant to go at it alone. (Hebrews 3:13; 11:24-25; 13:1, Proverbs 27:17, Psalms 133)
- Another form of apostasy is a result of mixed multitudes. Bad company corrupts good manners, teaches the Bible. A wise man once said, "what you look at, you end up looking like". This danger is ever-present as the church

has to have an open-door policy and believers also need to have the same - no church or believer should 'class' themselves such that they become unapproachable by people from outside the church. We can utilize umbrella policies and case-by-case review options not limited to rebuking, reforming, restricting, or rejecting in some circumstances. (1 and 2 Timothy)

- Apostasy can also be in the form of false teachings. From seemingly inconsequential doctrines to fringe belief systems (read Titus). Every new doctrine should build upon and be in line with what has been previously revealed. Test all spirits (1 John 4:1), verify all things (1 Thessalonians 5:21) and beware of false teachers. (Matthew 7:15)
- Apostasy also comes in forms inexhaustible in this short book, believers are endeared to continuously examine their doctrines as they

continue in the Christian journey. (1 Corinthians 10:12)

Deploying The DEA

- The actual DEA uses several detection methods to combat instances and chains of drug dealings. The Church and believers should also set up their own DEA policies and safeguards rooted in God and the Scriptures to prevent, find, and plug instances and chains of apostasy.

- Illicit drugs fester addiction through different means, apostasy is no different. It may seem non-dangerous, inconsequential, like a breath of fresh air, tickling to the ears, pseudo empowering, liberating, or even progressive. Do not be seduced or deceived, remember – DEA.

CHAPTER SIX
KGB (KILL GREED AND BOASTFULNESS)

t is perhaps an act of providence that this is a defunct acronym. Here, KGB stands for Kill(ing) Greed and Boastfulness, a treatment essential to Christian life and living. We seek medical treatment so that eventually we will not need it, e.g., we take medications so that we do not need to take anymore. In the same manner, Christians should deliberately eliminate and eradicate greed and boastfulness such that they are no longer issues that need to be addressed.

First, we must delineate what boastfulness is not. This is because it has become strangely popular to accuse religious peoples, especially Christians, of boastfulness or aggrandizement. It is not boastfulness:

- When Christians claim to possess the knowledge of God's existence - Job, a righteous man in many rights proclaims in Job 19:25-27, "I know that my redeemer lives..." To claim to know God exists is to admit that one is sinful and inadequate.

- When Christians lay claim to ultimate truth - It was Jesus who said, "I am the Way, the Truth and the Life..." (John 14:6). Christian claims to ultimate truth are a result of trusting the recorded words of Christ, and very few people will ascribe boastfulness to the person of Jesus.

- When Christians say that the God of the universe loves mankind and is interested in our affairs - Other than the intuitive and evidenced notion that the observable universe can be demonstrated to be immensely participant in the big picture propulsion of humanity, this issue has been contemplated by ancient and modern followers of God, "When I behold Your heavens, the work of Your fingers, the moon, and the stars, which You have set in place - what is man that You are mindful of him, or the son of man that You care for him? (Psalms 8:3-4)

- When Christians propagate the message of Christ around the world – No one intentionally hides something they consider as truth from those they care about. In fact, we proclaim truths to those we dislike and disagree with all the time. It is not arrogance, for example, to tell someone that fire is dangerous or that racism is wrong or that philanthropy is a beneficial ethic.

- When Christians describe their conceived ideas of events of the afterlife from scriptural knowledge when they attempt to lay out a prescription of how humans should conduct themselves based on the person of Jesus Christ, when they reject mainstream ideas of materialistic naturalism, or even when some Christians reject proposed theories of natural human evolution. Differing opinions do not automatically equal boastfulness.

It is unfortunately the case that boastfulness does indeed befall the Church and believers and we cannot exhaust the innumerable ways this can happen. Boastfulness will be used here as an umbrella term to include pride, arrogance, and their extended family. Greed here will also similarly be an umbrella term to include lust, discontent, covetousness, and their progeny as well.

Jesus said, "For all that is in the world, the lust of the flesh and the lust of the eyes and the boastful pride of life, is not from the Father, but is from the world. And the world passes away, and also its lusts, but the one who does the will of God abides forever." (1 John 2:16-17) And "Woe to you who are well fed now, for you will go hungry. Woe to you who laugh now, for you will mourn and weep." (Luke 5:25)

Swedish molecular biologist Dr. Jonas Frisen found in a widely accepted, repeated, and peer-reviewed study that all the cells of the body largely replace themselves every 7 to 10 years. Our present combination of cells would be dead and replaced in about a decade, along with their pride and desires. What abides is the identity we build over time, not what we have accrued, eaten, or enjoyed.

While Christians should indeed 'Kill Greed and Boastfulness' to eliminate the undesirable characteristics, to advocate or call for the abolishment of Christian religion because of the presence or prevalence of these traits is a non-sequitur; akin to saying that because many humans are murderous, all humanity should be eliminated. The snake does devour its own tail.

Deploying The KGB

- As mentioned earlier, the push to discard religion often comes armed with citations of these issues present in popular Christianity. This push can be resisted with humble acknowledgement of the situation, and the demonstrated effort to Kill off Greed and Boastfulness.
- The last five of the famous ten commandments can be used as foundational tenets when adopting this KGB acronym, "You shall not murder, … commit adultery, … steal, … lie, … covet…" (Exodus 20:13-17).
- Governing Christians should be the life and words of Jesus, who said to the disciples, "Take care, and be on your guard against all covetousness, for one's life does not consist in

the abundance of his possessions." and also, "Whoever wants to be first [in God's kingdom] must take the last place and be the servant of everyone else." (Mark 9:35)

CHAPTER SEVEN
GCHQ (GOD THE CHRIST HEADQUARTERS)

"Christ is also the head of the church, which is his body.
He is the beginning, supreme over all who rise from the
dead. So He is first in everything."
(Colossians 1:18)

All Christians everywhere should be registered active agents of the GCHQ, God the Christ Headquarters. The buck should start and stop with the person of Christ - the mission briefs and the after-action reports. Not only should Christians consider before actions, "What would Jesus do?" They should also ruminate after actions, "What would Jesus think and/or say?"

Due to the notoriety of the cynical sort of 'Kumbaya' and Hakuna Matata' unscriptural nonfactual ideations of Jesus in popular media, it is of utmost importance that Christians rely not on preconceived ideas but on a scripture-based personality of God who walked, ate, slept, suffered, underwent death and resurrection on the planet in the person of Jesus. One way to get this knowledge is to prayerfully and expectantly meditate on the four Gospels and other books of the canonical Bible.

Besetting the Church these days are the self - centered and transactional understandings of Christianity. The former generally teaches that God is there solely for the individual and all about them, to provide everything they want and more; while the later generally teaches that if the believer prays enough, have faith enough, church enough, then they get to enjoy the "la-la land American dream" of material abundance and that whenever they do not have these things, it's because they have not been faithful enough, prayerful enough, going to church enough, or 'sown' enough.

These understandings of Christianity are problematic and have been found at the center of what paints Christians in a bad, undesirable light.

Serving The GCHQ

- Instead of being a tool to search or rescue our faith and religion, GCHQ, the notion of God the Christ as HeadQuarters is well suited as an overarching and sovereign governing principle in our lives.

- God is not an unlimited personal genie at our every beck and call. We will only receive what we ask in His name as stated in John 14:13. God is also not singular about us as individuals, as Creator and Head of the Church, He is rather particular about everybody. (read John 3:16; 1 Timothy 2:4; 2 Peter 3:9)

- In Christ alone can we live a good and holy abundant life:
    - "Seek ye first the kingdom of God and His righteousness, and all these things [your needs] shall be added unto you." (Matthew 6:33)
    - "... for one's life does not consist in the abundance of his possessions." (Luke 12:15)
- It is true that in John 10:10, Jesus said to His followers, "I have come so that they may have life, and that they may have it abundantly." He also unequivocally defined what life is, saying:
    - "I am the resurrection and the life. Whoever believes in me, though he dies, yet shall he live," (John 11:25)

- "I am the way, and the truth, and the life. No one comes to the Father except through me." John (14:16) and

- "I am the bread of life; whoever comes to me shall not hunger, and whoever believes in me shall never thirst." (John 16:35)

Abundant Life in Christ is not as we see it, but as He sees it. We are promised all that we will need, not all that we want so that we can enjoy the best possible relationship with Him, now and in the life after.

Standard Operating Procedure

GCHQ, like every other organization, has its standard operating procedure, a list of tenets guiding Christian on how to easily carry out routinely complex operations. The Bible is an umbrella SOP and so in this book, the reader is treated to only a tiny fraction, in the hope that it will lead to more meditating on the wisdom contained in the entire book:

- Loving God with Everything, and loving our neighbor as ourselves, (Matthew 22:36-40)
- Loving and praying for our enemies and those who seek the opposite of our interests, (Luke 6: 27-36)
- Doing our best to be at peace with all men and living holy lives, (Romans 12:18; Hebrews 12:14)
- Living an exemplary lifestyle, such that people will see God through us, (Matthew 5:16)
- Focusing on heavenly things, and not earthly pleasures and possessions, (Colossians 3:2)
- Maintaining our beings in Christ by obeying His words and mapping our lives after His person, (John 15:4; Acts 17:28)
- Always striving for moral, physical, and spiritual perfection. (Matthew 5:48)

CHAPTER EIGHT

MISSION: IMPOSSIBLE – GHOST PROTOCOL

n the movie Mission: Impossible - Ghost Protocol, IMF agent Ethan Hunt purposely became incarcerated in a prison to acquire an item of high value, while another member of his team, Julia had to "die" and gain a new identity to ensure the overall success of the mission. Christians are also on a mission on earth, and we may need to deny ourselves of a lot of things, die to the world, and put on new identities for Jesus's Pearl of great price.

MISSION - The Christian mission echoes back to the very first chapter in the old testament, and even in the new testament, the look at three major mission objectives of Christians in the triad below:

I.   Repent and turn to God (Acts 3:19).

II.   Be ambassadors of Christ (2 Corinthians 5:20) - pleading with people in words and deeds to be reconciled to God.

III.   Make disciples of Christ (Matthew 28:19-20) - not our disciples, but Christ's disciples who obey His commandments!

GHOST PROTOCOL - like members of the IMF (in the Mission Impossible movies) in a faraway country, Christians are "in this world, but not of this world." Due to the unique nature of the Christian mission and its variable probability of success in a fallen world, a unique protocol is required to facilitate mission success:

I. Christ Himself invented and pioneered the ghost protocol, John 12:24-26; Mark 8:31.

II. In the same manner, though on a spiritual and internal level, we are to consider ourselves as dead to the world, Romans 6:11.

III. We do this by putting to death our earthly desires including "sexual immorality, impurity, lust, evil desires and greed, which is idolatry." (Colossians 3:5) this means that our scope of liberties become seemingly narrow.

(IM)POSSIBLE - There is an interesting motivational idea that the word 'impossible', when broken down, reads 'I'm possible". The seeming narrowing of liberties and constraints on Christian living may seem impossible, but it is not:

I. The first piece of good news is that it is something that we do not do alone, Christ explained that His death ushers in a helper who will teach us and bring to our remembrance all that we need to know. (John 14:26) Also,

II.   The protocol itself has already been jump-started for us, with the death of Christ as the energy or power source (1 Peter 2:24) and our baptism as the ignition (Romans 6:3), we just need to surrender into the process with the help of the Holy Spirit (2 Timothy 2:11; Colossians 3: 3-4). Lastly,

III.   However unlikely it may seem to be undertaken; nothing is impossible for God. If we trust and obey and rely on Him, we can have mission success. (Mark 10:27)

WIN-WIN SITUATION - Real or symbolic, we must all die someday. A popular Nigerian slang saying goes thus, "One thing must kill a man". The underhanded point is to encourage people to choose their "one thing" whenever they can and that they should not live in constant fear of death. Ghost protocol, though symbolic, has historically translated into real death and loss for many Christians. This is not bad news, because:

I. Earthly death is inevitable and incomparable to eternity "...To live is Christ, to die is gain" (Philippians 1:21). While we are to live as long as we can for the sake of Christ, we should be willing to give it up for His sake as well - as it is gainful.

II. There is more to life than comfort, luxury, and possessions. The majority of individuals who are most important to human history were those without any of the aforementioned. (Matthew 5:11-13)

III. "Sticks and stones may hurt my bones..." only God can harm the soul. Even when we face ardent opposition, we must still stay true to God as our souls are safe in His hands (John 10:28)

CHAPTER NINE

SEARCH AND RESCUE (PART 1)

"Let him who thinks he stands take care…"
(1 Corinthians 10:12)

Generally, Search and Rescue can be divided into two kinds – the rescue of uniformed personnel and civilian rescue. This Chapter is primarily related to the first kind, where the element that needs to be rescued is a part of the unit that is doing the rescuing. For example, when a team of marines goes rescue a marine, a uniformed member of the DOD, or some other member of the armed forces. This kind of rescue is relatively different because of the procedures followed.

This aspect of search and rescue for religious Christians in this chapter will cover personal, organizational, and communal search and rescue:

- **Personal** - By using the tools in the previous chapters and seeking appropriate help, Individual Christians are to inflect and search within themselves, aligning and realigning their religion closer to Christ; rescuing their religion from any entanglements that pose danger.

- **Organizational** - Using the same tools, Churches and Christian fellowships are to constantly monitor and comb through their religion - beliefs, doctrines, and teachings. The Holy Spirit is more than capable to rescue His Church from any danger that may lay in the tracks.

- **Communal** - Iron sharpens Iron, there are going to be times when other members of

Christ's family need to be there for one another. We should be the kind of family that is sensitive enough to timely recognize when one of us needs to be rescued from the fangs of the enemy. (John 13:35)

CHAPTER TEN

SEARCH AND RESCUE (PART 2)

Along with taking care of our own proverbial and actual 'household', the Great commission for Christians is to make disciples (Matthew 28:19-20). The making of disciples involves searching for and bringing in unbelievers from all corners of the earth into the body of Christ.

The second kind of Search and Rescue is the Civilian Rescue, when the element being rescued is not a part or affiliate of the rescuing group and may be unaware of their methods and procedures.

Civilian search and rescue for Christians can be further divided into two categories -

- **Actual Civilian** - This category encompasses all peoples who have always been unbelievers, including those who have heard the gospel and those who have never heard. (Matthew 10:18)

- **Ex-Military** - Or former believers. This second category encompasses every person who at one time or the other had been a member of the body of Christ but left the fold for one reason or another. (Luke 15:3-7)

In conclusion, Christians should search within and without, in a Spirit-led effort to rescue true religion and children of God (all humans) from the darkness of sin and ignorance. With the Word of God as our light, and His Truth as our rescuer, we can do it because our God Himself is a Master of Search and Rescue.

"For thus says the Lord God: Behold, I will search for my sheep and will seek them out. As a shepherd seeks out his flock when he is among his sheep that have been scattered, so will I seek out my sheep, and I will rescue them from all places where they have been scattered on a day of clouds and thick darkness."

(Ezekiel 34:11-12)

APPENDIX

Aggrandizement - to widen in scope; increase in size or intensity; enlarge; extend.

Akin - of similar character, similar.

Canonical - list of sacred books officially accepted as genuine.

Cartesian Certainty – Absolute certainty linked to Rene Descartes.

Coherence - the quality of being logical, consistent, and unified.

Delineate - to describe or portray (something) precisely.

Ergo - Latin for therefore.

Materialistic Naturalism - Naturalism is the view that the world can be explained entirely by physical, natural phenomena/laws. Materialism is the related view that all existence is matter, that only matter is real, and so that the world is just physical.

New Age Spirituality - New Age is a term applied to a range of spiritual or religious beliefs and practices that grew rapidly in the Western World during the 1970s, drawing heavily upon several older esoteric traditions.

New Apostolic Reformation - a movement that seeks to establish a fifth branch within Christendom, distinct from Catholicism, Protestantism, Oriental Orthodoxy, and Eastern Orthodoxy.

Non-sequitur - a conclusion or statement that does not logically follow from the previous argument or statement.

Normative - relating to, or deriving from, a standard or norm.

Polemic - a strong verbal or written attack on someone, something, an idea or ideology.

Pontification - To express opinions or judgments dogmatically.

Propagate - spread and promote (an idea, theory, etc.) widely.

Proliferation - the rapid increase in number or occurrence of something.

Purview - the scope of influence, experience, concerns, or thoughts.

Sobriety - clear-mindedness (being studious and logical), the state of not being under strange influence.

Synecdoche – a figure of speech using part of a thing to represent the whole or vice versa.

Transactional Christianity - a kind of tit for tat relationship, where you do for God so He can do for you.

Tenet - a principle or belief, especially one of the main principles of philosophy.

BIBLIOGRAPHY

- All Bible verses are of the English Standard Version and New International version. With permission.

- All definitions are excerpted from Merriam Webster dictionary and dictionary.com

- Cartesian Certainty – James Morris. "Cartesian Certainty". Australian Journal of philosophy. Volume 47 page 2.

- Encyclopedia of wars - Encyclopedia of Wars: G-R. Volume 2 of Encyclopedia of Wars, Charles Phillips, ISBN 0816028516, 9780816028511

- Information relating to the real meanings of acronyms used was gathered from public domain websites and platforms.

- "Mission impossible: Ghost Protocol" https://en.m.wikipedia.org/wiki/Mission:_Impossible_%E2%80%93_Ghost_Protocol

- Quotes of Ravi Zacharias -
  https://www.rzim.org/listen/let-my-people-think
- Spalding, K. L., Bhardwaj, R. D., Buchholz, B. A., Druid, H., & Frisén, J. (2005). Retrospective birth dating of cells in humans. Cell, 122(1), 133-143.
- Transactional Christianity- Faith meets World Online Journal
  http://www.faithmeetsworld.com/transactional-christianity/

AUTHOR'S NOTE

Thank you so much for reading my book!! I am grateful to God for bringing you to this point. This is not my first book, but it is the first completed and published work of mine. I hope you have been blessed and was able to catch a thing or two where it concerns your Religion, Christianity, and Faith in general. It honestly did not take me too long to write this book, what I was apparently waiting for was 2020!

So, what happened in 2020? Well, without mincing words, a global pandemic happened. This period highlighted the situation and created the time and opportunity. The pandemic of COVID-19 caused dynamic shifts and changes in the world of religion, with some cultures experiencing intensified religiosity and some cultures experiencing just the opposite.

There was however a curious general trend across the spectrum of the allure of take-over e-religion that seemed to be here to stay, compounding the mass exodus of the "un-churched" who have lost faith in the institution of church and congregation altogether. One way I saw to tackle this was to espouse the importance of the institution of religion while providing a means of cleaning up the mess that keeps repelling people from God-ordained religion, in my opinion. This was the groaning of my spirit that led to the wonderful short book you just finished!

Search and Rescue is at heart an expository piece and a call to action. It exposes the churched and non-churched alike to a different take on the idea and concept of religion (Christian religion specifically) and then goes on to call to action all concerned on sanitizing that religion and aligning it to the will and scriptural preference of the Author and Creator of Religion - God through Christ. Only God can lead man to God. Kindly pick up this book to read, again and again, endeavoring to read the passages quoted in context with solemnity, prayer, and expectancy.

Kindly send your reviews to

shore4nations@gmail.com where you will get a FREE E-book as your feedback is highly important to me and my team.

Thank you once again for picking up this book, stay blessed.

Joshua Sage
Author, Search and Rescue

He can be reached via:

Gmail: dukejoshmaser@gmail.com

Twitter: https://twitter.com/Apostle_sage

Facebook: https://web.facebook.com/adeyanju.josh

Instagram: https://www.instagram.com/apostle_sage/

www.ingramcontent.com/pod-product-compliance
Lightning Source LLC
Chambersburg PA
CBHW060454160726
47992CB00003B/1213